Minibeasts

Lynn Huggins-Cooper

Illustrated by

Shelagh McNicholas
David Burroughs

FRANKLIN WATTS
LONDON • SYDNEY

About the author
Lynn Huggins-Cooper is a
lecturer in primary science
at Newcastle University and
specialises in interactive
teaching methods. She also
creates wildlife gardens for
schools and runs a
conservation club.

First published in 2003 by Franklin Watts
96 Leonard Street, London EC2A 4XD

Franklin Watts Australia
45-51 Huntley Street
Alexandria, NSW 2015

Series editor: Rachel Cooke
Art director: Jonathan Hair
Design: James Marks

A CIP catalogue record for this book is
available from the British Library.

ISBN 0 7496 4859 7

Printed in Hong Kong, China

Contents

Ellie is going on a minibeast hunt! Come with her and see what she finds.

Ladybird, ladybird

Ellie has found a ladybird on a sweet-smelling rose bush.

There are lots of different kinds of ladybird.

Some have two spots.

Some have seven spots.

Some have 22 spots!

A ladybird is an **insect**. It has six legs. Can you count them?

Aphids get their food by sucking out the juices from roses and other plants. This damages the plants.

Ladybirds eat the aphids, so they help to protect the plants.

Look! The ladybird is eating an aphid – a tiny green insect. It eats thousands of these during its life.

Why do you think gardeners like ladybirds?

Ellie has found something else. The ladybird has laid some custard-yellow eggs on a leaf.

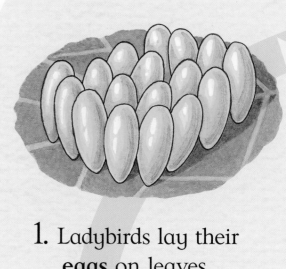

1. Ladybirds lay their **eggs** on leaves.

5. The ladybird breaks out of the case. It is now fully-grown. Its colour will darken in a couple of days.

2. When a baby ladybird hatches, it doesn't look like a ladybird! Its skin is black and looks like a rubber tyre.

What other animal babies look very different from their parents? Does Ellie look like her family?

3. The baby ladybirds eat aphids too. They shed their skins several times as they grow.

4. The baby ladybird's last skin dries to form a hard case. It is changing inside...

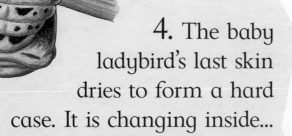

Ellie shows her mum and her sister Beth what she has found.

Beautiful butterflies

Ellie has spotted some colourful butterflies.

Butterflies are insects and there are lots of different types. Here are some Ellie has seen:

Cabbage white

Red admiral

Common blue

Peacock

The big marks on a Peacock butterfly's wings look like eyes. This scares away birds who might eat them!

Ellie is thirsty. She has a drink while she watches the butterfly drink nectar from a flower.

A butterfly uses its hollow tongue like a straw to drink **nectar**.

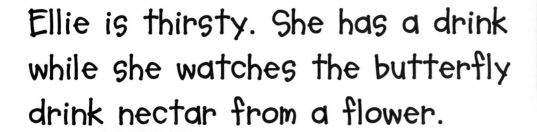

When it's finished drinking, its tongue rolls up like a tiny party blower.

Nectar is a sugary liquid made by flowers. Insects like to drink it. Bees make honey from nectar.

Mum is helping Ellie look for butterfly eggs among the nettles.

Careful, Ellie! Nettles can sting you!

1. A Peacock butterfly lays its eggs on a nettle leaf.

6. The butterfly dries its wings in the sun. When they are dry, it can fly away.

Why do you think nettles are a good place for a butterfly to lay its eggs?

Look back at pages 8 and 9 and see how a ladybird changes as it grows. Does a butterfly change in the same way?

2. When the babies hatch, they don't look like butterflies! They are black and velvety. The babies are called **caterpillars**.

3. A caterpillar munches leaves, and grows quickly.

5. When the butterfly hatches, it pushes its way out of the case like you pushing out of a tight sleeping bag.

4. One day, a caterpillar spins a case round itself. The case is called a **chrysalis**. Inside, the caterpillar is changing.

13

Darting dragonflies

Ellie and Beth are watching dragonflies flitting around the pond.

Dragonflies are insects. Beth and Ellie are watching an Emperor dragonfly.

Dragonfly

Damselfly

A damselfly is another insect that looks a bit like a dragonfly.

Dragonflies' wings have a network of veins in them. They look like delicate lace!

Dragonflies eat other small insects. Here are some of them:

Midge

Mosquito

Mayfly

Ellie doesn't like itchy midges. The dragonfly does, though! It catches the tiny flying insects in the air, and then eats them.

How many legs do insects have?

15

Beth and Ellie are looking at nymphs! These are baby dragonflies and they live underwater.

Don't **nymphs** look like alien monsters?

A dragonfly lays her eggs in the pond.

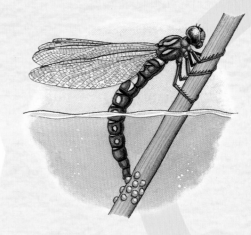

If it is scared, the nymph can move quickly by squirting a jet of water out of its tail, like a supersoaker water pistol!

The nymphs hatch out under the water.

We call the different stages of an animal's life a **life cycle**. These pictures show a dragonfly's life cycle. Point at its different stages in the correct order.

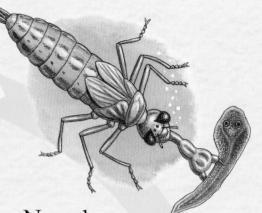

Nymphs are fierce hunters. They even eat tadpoles and small fish.

A glittering dragonfly crawls out.

After a short while, its skin splits.

After two years or longer, the nymph crawls up a plant stem, out of the water.

17

Spinning spiders

Ellie has found a Tiger spider. Its beautiful, silky web sparkles with dew.

Spiders have eight legs. There are lots of different types of spider. Here are a few:

Zebra spider

Wolf spider

Tiger spider

Crab Spider

? ? ?

A spider has eight legs. How does this tell us it is not an insect?

Spiders eat insects. This one has caught a wasp in its sticky web. It wraps it in silk to eat later.

Some spiders, like the Wolf spider, don't spin a web. Instead, they hunt for their food.

Spiders spin their **webs** from silk they make in their bodies.

Spiders build different types of web.

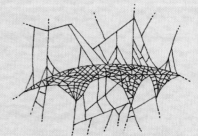

Orb web

Hammock web

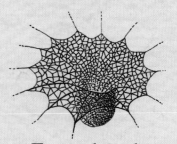

Funnel web

Ellie has found something hidden on the fence. It's a tiny white silk pom-pom. Safely inside it are a spider's eggs.

Why do you think the spider wraps her eggs in silk?

20

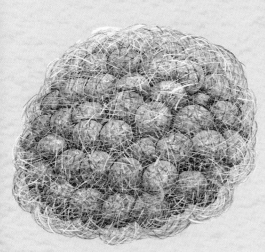

1. The spider makes a soft bag of silk, called a **sac**. She lays her eggs inside it.

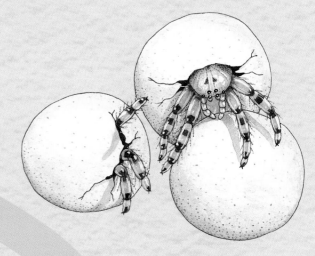

2. When the babies hatch, they are perfect tiny spiders.

Spiders help farmers. They eat many of the insects that can damage crops.

3. The baby spiders spread out to find food. They spin silken threads and float away on the wind.

4. When the spiders land, they begin to make webs of their own.

Slithering snails

Ellie's been turning over stones! She has found some worms, some woodlice and lots of snails.

Snails hide wherever it is damp and dark. Here are some places to look for them:

Under stones

In plant pots

Among thick leaves

A snail has a rough tongue so it can scrape bits off leaves and eat them.

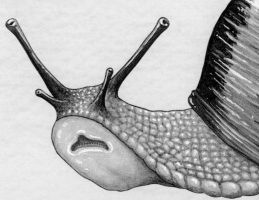

A snail has four feelers or **tentacles**. The snail's eyes are at the end of the two longer tentacles.

???

Ellie's snails have been busy eating leaves. Look at the lacy holes they have made.

Why do you think gardeners don't like snails?

Ellie is hunting for more snails. She follows the silvery trails they leave behind them.

Snails have no legs. They move around by making a thin layer of slime which they use to slide their bodies along.

When the slime dries, it forms a silvery trail.

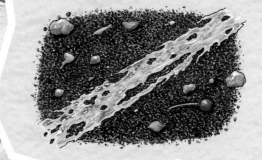

Follow the trails of Ellie's snails. How many snails can you find?

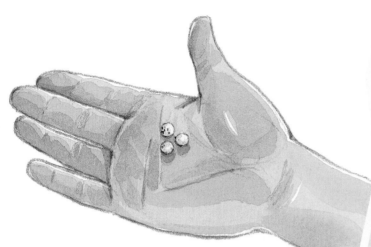

1. A snail lays its eggs in the soil.

Beth has found some snail's eggs for Ellie. They look like milky white bubbles.

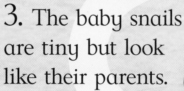

2. After a few weeks, the snails begin to hatch.

3. The baby snails are tiny but look like their parents.

Why do you think snails have shells? Trace the shell's spiral shape with your finger.

4. As they grow, snails' shells get bigger and have more spirals.

Find the minibeast

There are lots more minibeasts for Ellie to find. Hunting bugs is fun!

These are some minibeasts that Ellie has missed. Can you find them in the picture?

Worm

Beetle

Can you spot the minibeasts Ellie has already seen? What are their names?

Slug

Fly

Moth

Wasp

Bee

Centipede

Try this yourself!

Have some minibeast fun.

Follow that snail

Put a snail carefully on a clear plastic tray so you can see it slither from below. Watch it ripple as it moves! Alternatively, lift a slug or snail carefully on to black paper and let it move along. It will leave behind a silvery trail!

At home in the trees

Find out what's living in a tree - you'll be amazed! Spread a white sheet under a small, leafy tree and gently shake the tree's trunk. What drops out?

Once you've identified your finds, leave the sheet out for a while so the minibeasts can climb back into their tree.

A minibeast's diary

Use what you have learned from this book to help you to write the diary of a minibeast - and make it minibeast-shaped. Fold up a large piece of paper into a fan. Draw a minibeast shape on one side, making sure it touches the two upright edges. Cut it out carefully. It should make a paper-chain book which you can fill in.

Useful words

caterpillar: A baby butterfly, which looks very different from the fully-grown butterfly.

chrysalis: The case a caterpillar makes when it is changing into a fully-grown butterfly.

eggs: Eggs are laid by many animals, such as insects and birds. Their babies hatch from them.

insect: A type of animal with six legs. Insects often change a lot during their life cycle.

life cycle: The way an animal grows and changes through its life.

nectar: A sugary liquid made by flowers. Many insects feed on nectar.

nymph: A baby dragonfly, which looks very different from the fully-grown dragonfly.

sac: The tiny silk bag spun by a spider to hold its eggs.

tentacles: The long feelers of certain animals, including snails and slugs.

web: Spiders spin webs with their silk to trap the animals that they eat.

About this book

This book encourages children to explore and discover science in their local, familiar environment - in the garden or at the park. By starting from 'where they are', it aims to increase children's knowledge and understanding of the world around them, encouraging them to examine objects and living things closely and from a more scientific perspective.

Familiar minibeasts are looked at in turn, focusing on feeding, habitat and life cycle. Questions are asked to build on children's natural curiosity and encourage them to think about what they are reading. Some questions send children back to the book to find the answers, others point to new ideas that, through discussion, the readers may 'discover' for themselves.

Index